Hanako's Egg

Written by Mio Debnam

Illustrated by Yu Kito Lee

Collins

1 The egg

Hanako visits Garden Farm. Hanako and her dad love it. Her mum is not keen.

Some animals come up for a look.

That night, there is a gift in Hanako's bag.

"Can we keep it to see if a chick comes out?"
Hanako asks.

Dad agrees.

2 Cheep the chick

Hanako waits and waits. Then a little chick bursts out of the shell.

"Do not let Tora hurt it," Mum insists.

But Tora the cat loves the chick.
Cheep grooms Tora's fur.

Tora and Cheep trail Hanako. They do not let her go far!

3 The hen house

Cheep will soon be a hen.

Hanako puts up a hen house in the back garden for Cheep to sleep in.

"That chicken needs to be on a farm!"
Mum moans.

"Just look at this mess!" she adds.

Hanako puts fresh bedding in the hen house.

Cheep loves sleeping in the snug dark nest.

One morning, Cheep starts clucking.

Hanako runs to the garden in alarm.

Cheep is sitting on the bag Hanako took to the farm.

In the bag is an egg.

"You did it, Cheep!" yells Hanako.

Hanako cooks Mum tamago-yaki — an egg
dish from Japan.

"This is good!" Mum tells Hanako. "Cheep is turning out to be a star chicken!"

"Good job, Cheep!" grins Hanako. "You can keep my bag."

Hanako and Cheep

Buck
Buck

 After reading

Letters and Sounds: Phases 3 and 4

Word count: 233

Focus phonemes: /ch/ /sh/ /th/ /ng/ /ai/ /ee/ /igh/ /oa/ /oo/ /oo/ /ar/ /or/ /ur/, and adjacent consonants

Common exception words: of, to, the, no, go, puts, my, she, we, me, be, you, they, do, some, come, there, little, one, out, house, asks, love, her

Curriculum links: Science: Animals, including humans; Design and technology: Cooking and nutrition

National Curriculum learning objectives: Reading/word reading: apply phonic knowledge and skills as the route to decode words; read accurately by blending sounds in unfamiliar words containing GPCs that have been taught; Reading/comprehension (KS2): develop positive attitudes to reading and understanding of what they have read by discussing words and phrases that capture the reader's interest and imagination; understand what they read, in books they can read independently, by: checking that the text makes sense to them, discussing their understanding and explaining the meaning of words in context; asking questions to improve their understanding of a text; drawing inferences such as inferring characters' feelings, thoughts and motives from their actions

Developing fluency

- Take turns to read a page, ensuring your child pauses briefly at the dash on page 19 and understands that this helps with comprehension.
- Encourage your child to read with expression, using different voices for each character.

Phonic practice

- Practise reading words with adjacent consonants:
  trail   bursts   gift   still
- Challenge your child to read these two-syllable words with adjacent consonants: agrees   sleeping   morning   clucking

Extending vocabulary

- Point to **not keen** on page 2. Can your child think of two words to describe how Mum is feeling? (e.g. *nervous, bored*)
- Take turns to think of two "feelings" words for characters on other pages.